A GIFT FOR:

_____

FROM:

_____

Published in 2019 by Hallmark Gift Books, a
division of Hallmark Cards, Inc., under license from
Chronicle Books. Visit us on the web at Hallmark.com.

Chronicle Books LLC
680 Second Street
San Francisco, CA 94107
www.chroniclebooks.com

Chronicle Books publishes distinctive books and gifts.
From award-winning children's titles, best-selling
cookbooks, and eclectic pop culture to acclaimed
works of art and stationery, and journals, we craft
publishing that's instantly recognizable for its spirit
and creativity. Enjoy our publishing and become part
of our community at www.chroniclebooks.com.

1BOK1436
ISBN: 978-1-63059-666-8

Made in China

NAME *That* MOVIE

50 Illustrated Movie Puzzles

by PAUL ROGERS

Hallmark

CHRONICLE BOOKS
SAN FRANCISCO

INTRODUCTION

While watching *Chinatown* for about the fiftieth time—during the scene when Gittes places two watches under the tire of Hollis Mulwray's car—it occurred to me that if I made a drawing of the watches and the tire, people who love the movie would recognize that small moment in the film. This led to the idea that a series of drawings made from classic films might make an interesting visual quiz.

Soon, I began re-watching some of my favorite movies with a sketchbook and pausing the film to make drawings. For the most part, I tried to avoid the most obvious scenes and stars who might give away the title too easily and instead, concentrated on details that appealed to me. As a graphic designer who particularly loves architecture and typography, I found myself paying close attention to buildings and signs. Also, lettering—large or small—always jumped out at me. I hadn't noticed until I started working on this book how frequently handwritten notes or pieces of printed paper appear as important elements of the plot.

I found that six drawings in sequence could give a nice sense of the film. The goal was to give hints that spark the memory of a film rather than tell the whole story.

Of course, some of the movies had dozens of great shots for drawings and it was a challenge to pick just six, while others required much deeper scrutiny.

The movies in this book are all films that I love. Some of them I'm certain everyone has seen, while others may have slipped from public awareness; but they're all great. There's a lot of Hitchcock (hint), and Billy Wilder, some vintage film noir and recent box office hits, a few foreign films, and somehow, a lot of films from the seventies. Some of my favorite movies didn't make the cut because they might be a little too obscure to work well in this puzzle context (hard to guess a film you haven't seen or heard of), but I will say that if you haven't seen *Pickup on South Street* (1953) and *Elevator to the Gallows* (1958) you should!

There are one hundred movies in this book. The answers are given in two places in the back. There's a list of titles in the order that they appear in the book and there's also an alphabetical index. The alphabetical index is there for readers who don't want to inadvertently see the next title on the list when checking the answers. I hope you enjoy the book and find yourself paying a bit more attention to those small moments that make up great films.

I'd like to add a word of appreciation to my wife Jill, who tolerated a lot of Sunday afternoons while I sat on the sofa in front of the television with a sketchbook and the remote control. Now that the book's finished, we can go out on Sundays and maybe see a movie.

—*Paul Rogers*

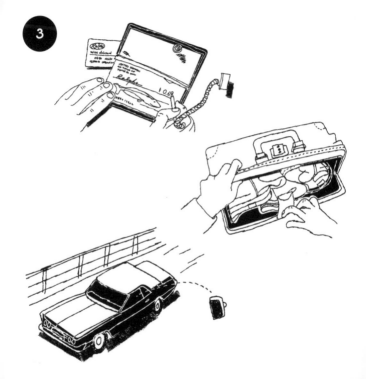

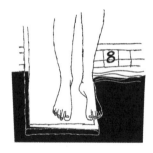

SENIOR PICNIC OR BUST
ANARENE HIGH 1952

DIVISION of CORRECTIONS
ROAD PRISON 36

Exhibit A
1428

REAL ESTATE

SEE
WALLY FAY
FOR BEST BUYS IN
REAL ESTATE

WALLY FAY

LOTS ·HOUSES
RENTALS
INSURANCE

Society and Clubs

Ladies Guild
to Give Buffet
Luncheon

Business Woman,
Beragon Heir Wed

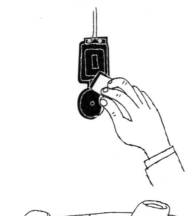

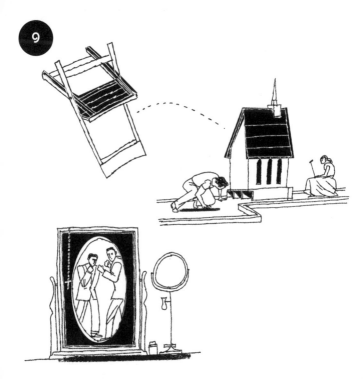

DEBONAIR
SOCIAL CLUB

MEMBERS ONLY

An Evening WITH
JAKE LA MOTTA
featuring the works of
• PADDY CHAYEFSKY
• ROD SERLING
• SHAKESPEARE
• BUDD SCHULBERG
• TENNESSEE WILLIAMS
Tonight

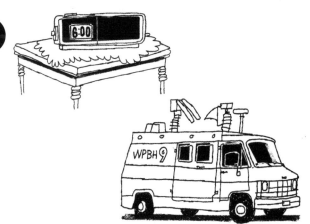

11

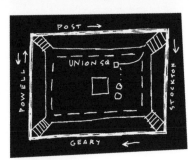

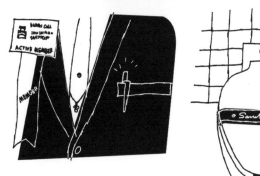

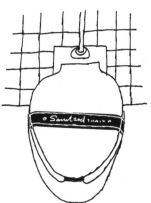

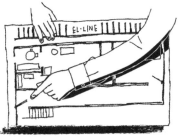

STEP

DRAG . . .

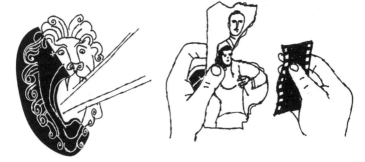

16

Elaine's

पाश्चात्य शैली
WESTERN STYLE

VOLTAIRE #6
Le Parfum Art

PARIS

DIME AND SPY
INCORPORATED

SIDNEY KIDD
EDITOR AND PUBLISHER

CLICK

PUBLIC LIBRARY
OPEN DAILY

9 AM to 5 PM
WED. EVENINGS
7 PM to 8 PM

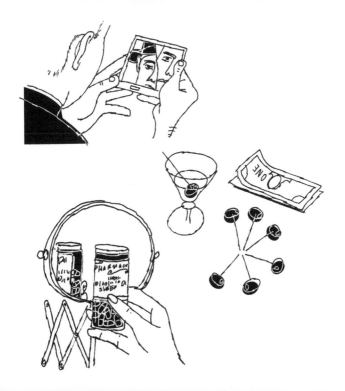

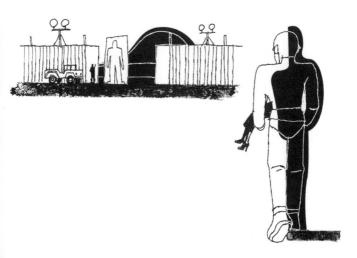

STAGE · BROADWAY · SCREEN

VARIETY
25 CENTS

STUDIOS CONVERT TO TALKIES

| BEST RESTAURANT ON B'WAY STARTS ON SHOESTRING | MAD SCRAMBLE ON FOR SOUND | SOCK BIZ FOR LEGIT NOW BUT MOVIE'S STILL STIFF |

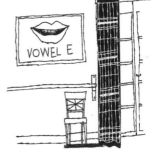

VOWEL E

HOTEL ASTOR · STRAND · SARDI'S · Casino · PALACE · Gaiety · LOEW'S · LOEW'S STATE · CRITERION · ASTOR HOTEL

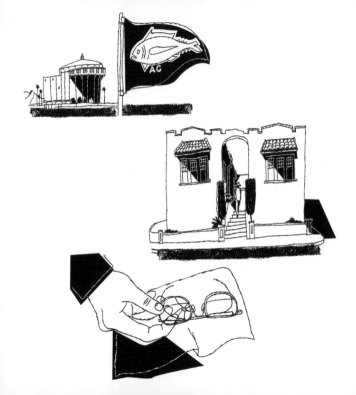

25

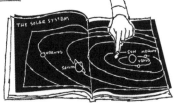

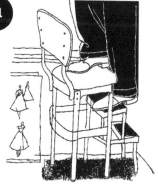

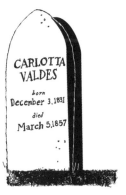

CARLOTTA
VALDES

born
December 3, 1831

died
March 5, 1857

32

THE SORROW AND THE PITY
©CINEMA 5 LTD. 1972
©MARCEL OPHULS, ANDRE HARRIS, 1969

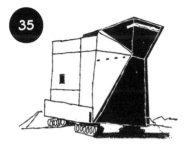

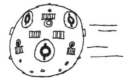

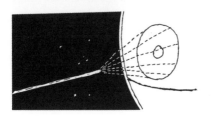

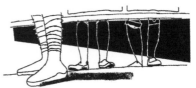

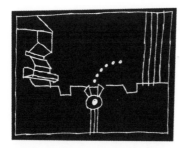

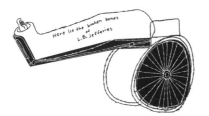

Here lie the broken bones of L.B. Jefferies

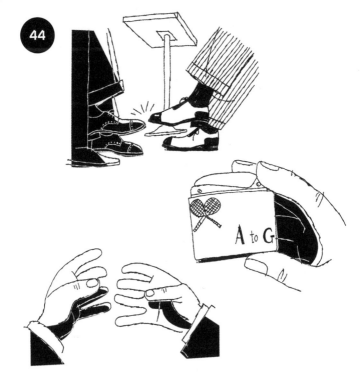

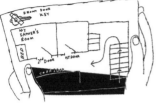

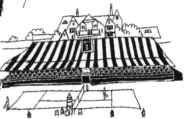

CHET!

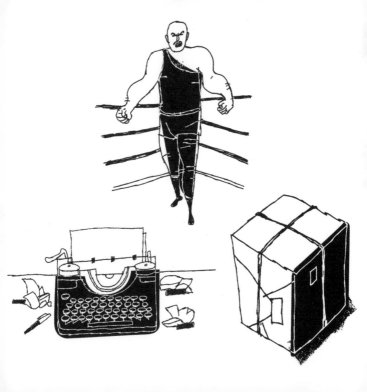

3 Years Dead

H.J. DELBRUCK

Bucharest Academy of Science
TONIGHT ONLY
DR. F. FRANKENSTEIN
PRESENTS
THE CREATURE
IN
"A Startling New Experiment in Re..."
PRESENTED IN COOPERATION WITH TNS
(Transylvania Ne...)

SOLD OUT

ANSWERS

1 Casablanca (1942)

7 Mildred Pierce (1945)

2 Zoolander (2001)

8 Double Indemnity (1944)

3 The Big Lebowski (1998)

9 Raging Bull (1980)

4 The Last Picture
Show (1971)

10 Groundhog Day (1993)

5 The Graduate (1967)

11 Citizen Kane (1941)

6 Cool Hand Luke (1967)

12 The Conversation (1974)

13 12 Angry Men (1957)

14 Sweet Smell of Success (1957)

15 Cinema Paradiso (1988)

16 Manhattan (1979)

17 The Darjeeling Limited (2007)

18 The Philadelphia Story (1940)

19 The Apartment (1960)

20 Midnight Cowboy (1969)

21 The Day the Earth Stood Still (1951)

22 Singin' in the Rain (1952)

23 Do the Right Thing (1989)

24 Chinatown (1974)

25 Breathless (1960)

26 The Red Shoes (1948)

27 Sunset Blvd. (1950)

28 E.T.: The Extra-Terrestrial (1982)

29 Pee-Wee's Big Adventure (1985)

30 Raiders of the Lost Ark (1981)

31 Vertigo (1958)

32 Dog Day Afternoon (1975)

33 Annie Hall (1977)

34 Ferris Bueller's Day Off (1986)

35 Star Wars: Episode IV – A New Hope (1977)

36 La Dolce Vita (1960)

37 Rear Window (1954)

38 Three Days of the Condor (1975)

39 O Brother, Where Art Thou? (2000)

40 Broadway Danny Rose (1984)

41 Diner (1982)

42 Guys and Dolls (1955)

43 Monty Python and the Holy Grail (1974)

44 Strangers on a Train (1951)

45 To Kill a Mockingbird (1962)

46 The 39 Steps (1935)

47 The Umbrellas of Cherbourg (1964)

48 Barton Fink (1991)

MOVIE INDEX